Civilian to GUARDIAN

by Meish Goldish

Consultant: Fred Pushies
U.S. SOF Adviser

BEARPORT PUBLISHING
New York, New York

Credits

Cover and Title Page, © U.S. Coast Guard/PA3 Matthew Belson and U.S. Coast Guard/PA2 Nathan Henise; 4, © U.S. Coast Guard/Petty Officer 2nd Class Etta Smith; 5, © U.S. Coast Guard; 6, © U.S. Coast Guard; 7, © U.S. Coast Guard; 8, © U.S. Coast Guard/PAC Tom Sperduto; 9, © U.S. Coast Guard; 10, © U.S. Coast Guard/PAC Tom Sperduto; 11L, © U.S. Coast Guard/Petty Officer 2nd Class Christopher D. McLaughlin; 11R, © U.S. Coast Guard; 12, © U.S. Coast Guard; 13, © U.S. Coast Guard; 14L, © U.S. Coast Guard; 14R, © U.S. Coast Guard; 15T, © U.S. Coast Guard; 15B, © U.S. Coast Guard; 16T, © U.S. Coast Guard; 16B, © U.S. Coast Guard; 17, © U.S. Coast Guard; 18, © U.S. Coast Guard/PAC Tom Gillespie; 19, © U.S. Coast Guard; 20, © U.S. Coast Guard/Petty Officer 2nd Class Christopher D. McLaughlin; 21L, © U.S. Coast Guard photo by Petty Officer 3rd Class Robert Brazzell; 21R, © Yuri Gripas/Reuters/Landov; 22, © U.S. Coast Guard/Petty Officer Pamela J. Manns.

Publisher: Kenn Goin
Senior Editor: Lisa Wiseman
Creative Director: Spencer Brinker
Design: Debrah Kaiser
Photo Researcher: Daniella Nilva

Library of Congress Cataloging-in-Publication Data

Goldish, Meish.
Coast Guard : civilian to guardian / by Meish Goldish ; consultant, Fred Pushies.
p. cm. — (Becoming a soldier)
Includes bibliographical references and index.
ISBN-13: 978-1-936088-12-6 (library binding)
ISBN-10: 1-936088-12-6 (library binding)
1. United States. Coast Guard—Juvenile literature. I. Pushies, Fred J., 1952- II. Title.
VG53.G65 2011
363.28'6—dc22

2010011124

For more information, write to Bearport Publishing Company, Inc., 101 Fifth Avenue, Suite 6R, New York, New York 10003. Printed in the United States of America in North Mankato, Minnesota.

072010
042110CGD

10 9 8 7 6 5 4 3 2 1

Contents

Fire Drill 4

A New Recruit 6

A Noisy Start 8

The Company Commander 10

Getting into Shape 12

Class Time 14

Gun Training 16

Put to the Test 18

Graduation Day 20

Preparing for the Coast Guard 22

Glossary 23

Index 24

Bibliography 24

Read More 24

Learn More Online 24

About the Author 24

Fire Drill

As a fire burned out of control aboard a boat, a team of men and women struggled with heavy water hoses. They needed to drag them close enough to the raging flames to **douse** the fire. When they finally got into position, they sprayed gallons and gallons of water until the last of the flames died out. All that remained was thick, dark smoke.

A team getting ready to put out a fire

Luckily, this was not a real emergency. It was part of a training exercise for **seaman recruits** in the U.S. **Coast Guard**. The **drill** was a way for recruits such as John Patrone to learn that a **Guardian** must always be ready for any kind of emergency at sea.

Recruits wear protective uniforms during firefighting drills.

The Coast Guard is a branch of the **armed forces** that protects the nation's coasts and comes to the aid of boats and ships that are in trouble.

A New Recruit

There was no doubt in John Patrone's mind that he wanted to serve in this branch of the armed forces. He says that he had always "had his heart set on piloting a boat for the Coast Guard." He thought it would be exciting to rescue boaters who were **stranded** in storms. He especially looked forward to becoming part of one of the most important **nautical** groups in the world.

Seaman recruit John Patrone

After **enlisting**, John reported to the Coast Guard Training Center in Cape May, New Jersey, for basic training. This is an intense and grueling eight-week program that all recruits must go through. During this time, they learn how to perform rescues at sea as well as stop terror attacks and drug **smuggling** along U.S. coasts.

The Coast Guard Training Center at Cape May, New Jersey

● Location of the Coast Guard Training Center

The Coast Guard Training Center in Cape May, New Jersey, is the place where all **civilians**, men and women, go for basic Coast Guard training.

A Noisy Start

New recruits get a taste of what their basic training will be like within moments of arriving at Cape May by bus. As soon as the doors open, a Coast Guard officer starts shouting, "You've got ten seconds to get off this bus, and you've just wasted three!"

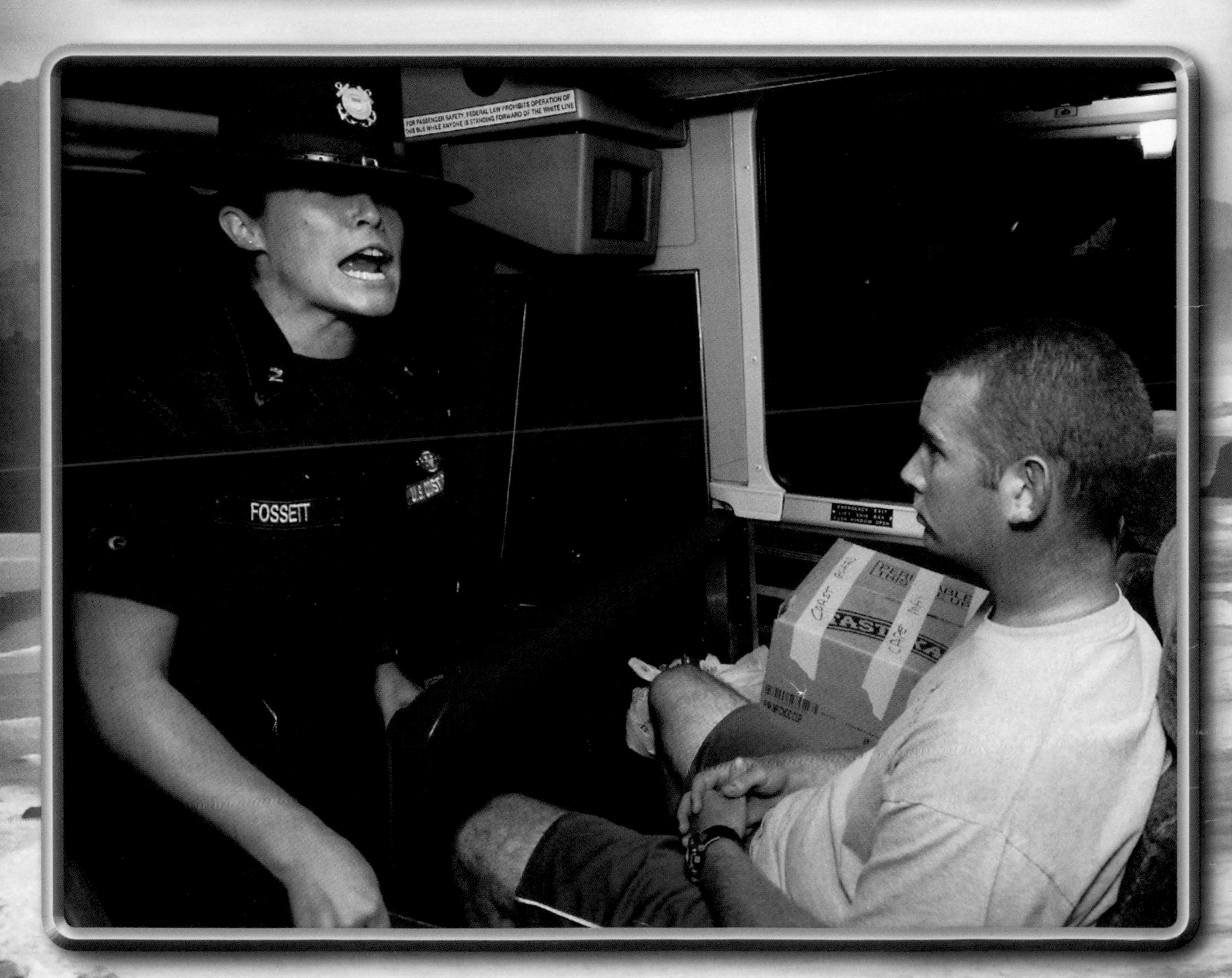

A Coast Guard officer shouts at a busload of recruits who have just arrived at Cape May.

During the next few days, the recruits are busy going through a series of activities called **processing**. Orders are yelled at them while they're given medical exams and are tested for drugs. They also receive their uniforms and fill out piles of paperwork. Everything the recruits do must be done quickly because they are given only a short amount of time to complete each task.

Officers shout at new recruits to get them used to obeying orders as a group. The Coast Guard wants the recruits to stop thinking like individuals and to start thinking like they are part of a team.

An officer yells at a new recruit.

The Company Commander

After processing, recruits are placed into a group called a **company**. It usually has about 50 to 60 members and includes both men and women. A company **commander** is in charge of the group for the rest of basic training.

A company commander giving his new recruits instructions

Recruits must always address their company commander as "Sir" or "Ma'am" at both the start and the end of a sentence. For example, a recruit answering yes to a question would say, "Sir, yes, sir!"

Company commanders, or CCs, have two main jobs. They teach recruits how to obey orders and also how to work as a team. For example, the company often marches together as a group. CCs are quick to yell at any recruit who makes a mistake, such as not marching at the same **pace** as everyone else. Often, CCs order recruits to do push-ups or sit-ups as punishment for their mistakes.

A recruit doing push-ups as a punishment for a mistake

A company commander yells at a recruit who failed to follow orders correctly.

Getting into Shape

A big part of basic training for the recruits involves physical **conditioning**. Recruits start their day very early—at about 5:30 in the morning. They are given just ten minutes to eat breakfast. Then the company commander leads them through an exhausting workout that includes running, push-ups, and sit-ups. Even when their muscles start to ache, the recruits aren't allowed to stop. They must keep going. The workout lasts for about an hour.

Recruits exercise in order to become as quick and strong as they can by the time they graduate.

Later on in the day, recruits practice water survival skills. These are important to Guardians because part of their job is rescuing others at sea. There is also always the chance that they themselves might fall overboard. That is why a lot of time is spent on swimming drills that include diving, racing, floating, and **treading** water.

Recruits must be able to swim 100 meters (109 yards) in five minutes. Those who can't swim when they enter the Coast Guard are taught how during basic training. However, the Coast Guard discourages anyone who is afraid of the water from joining this branch of the armed forces.

Recruits practice treading water.

Class Time

Basic training is more than just physical training. Recruits spend much of their day taking classes. They study the history and rules of the Coast Guard. They also take hands-on courses to learn how to **navigate** a boat or ship, tie rope knots, fight ship fires, and perform first aid.

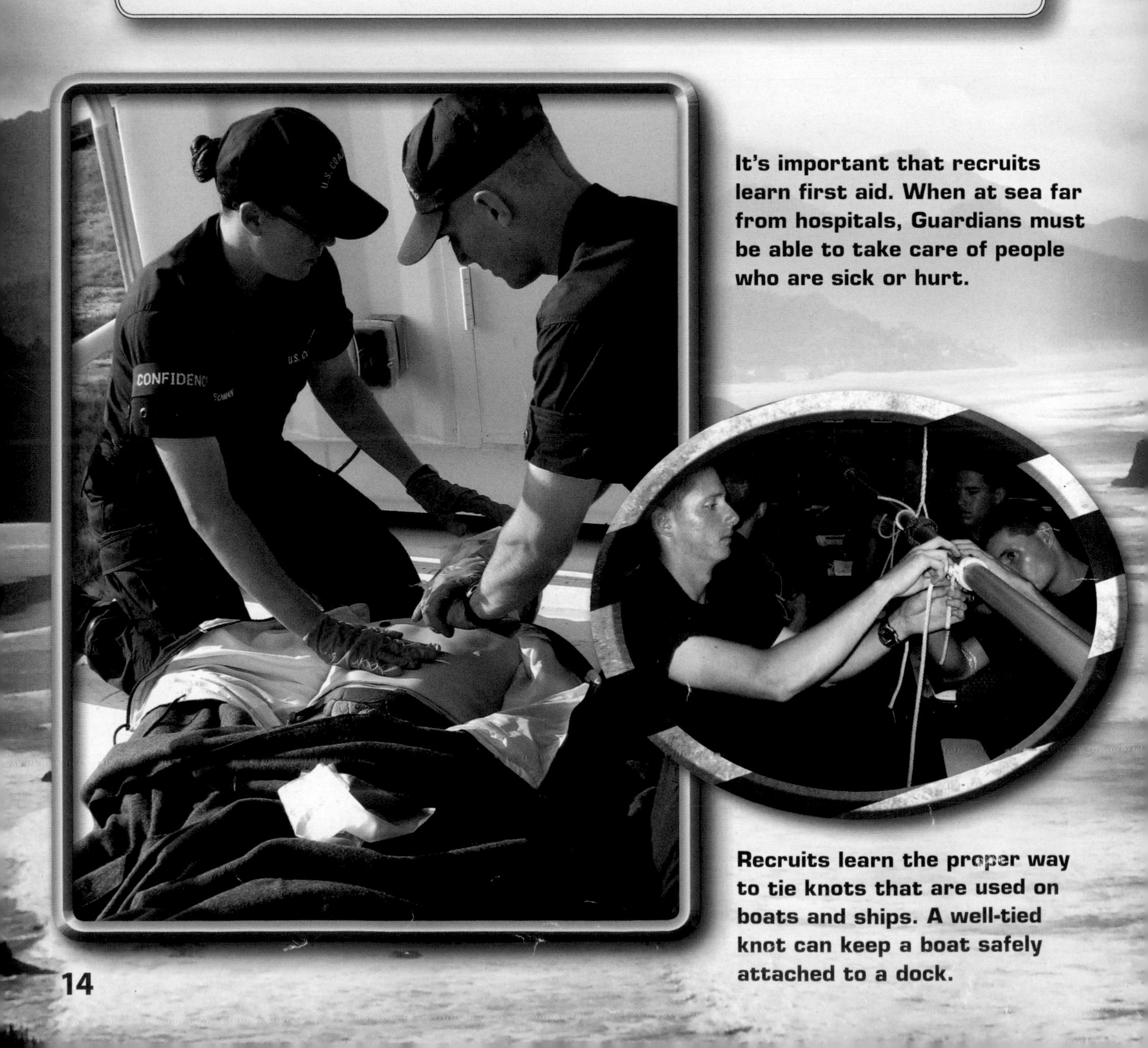

It's important that recruits learn first aid. When at sea far from hospitals, Guardians must be able to take care of people who are sick or hurt.

Recruits learn the proper way to tie knots that are used on boats and ships. A well-tied knot can keep a boat safely attached to a dock.

Recruits hardly have a second to relax. Outside of taking classes, they are expected to study a book called *The Helmsman*. This guide explains things such as the meaning of nautical terms and the various Coast Guard officer **ranks**. Recruits must pass a written test on all the information in the book before they can graduate.

Recruits spend a part of their day learning about the history of the U.S. Coast Guard.

In class, recruits learn about the three main Coast Guard values: honor, respect, and devotion to duty. Honor means never lying, cheating, or stealing. Respect means treating all people fairly and equally. Devotion to duty means doing the job of a Guardian in a responsible way. Recruits are expected to live by these values—both in basic training and for the rest of their lives.

Recruits must memorize information in the book *The Helmsman*.

Gun Training

During basic training, recruits are taught the importance of using a gun. Guardians need to know how to use one because while they're policing the U.S. coasts they may come face to face with criminals carrying weapons. As part of their training, recruits learn how to fire the Sig Sauer P229 **pistol**. It's a small gun that delivers a powerful shot.

A recruit learning how to aim her gun properly

Sig Sauer P229 pistol

Recruits are taught more than just how to fire their weapons. They're trained to load, unload, and clean them as well. They drill for hours at a time, until their fingers are sore. Recruits learn that a clean gun can save their lives because it's unlikely to misfire or jam when used.

Among their duties, Guardians search boats and ships that may be carrying illegal drugs or hiding people who are barred from entering the United States. Guardians must be ready to use their guns on criminals who might attack them.

Recruits spend many hours firing their guns.

Put to the Test

Before recruits can graduate from basic training, they are tested on everything they've learned while at Cape May. They are given a written exam and must take a physical fitness test as well as a swimming test. Recruits who fail any of these exams may be forced to repeat part or all of their basic training.

Seaman recruits taking a written exam

For their physical fitness test, men must run 1.5 miles (2.4 km) in under 12 minutes and 51 seconds. Women must complete the run in under 15 minutes and 26 seconds. Men must do 29 push-ups and 38 sit-ups, each set in one minute. Women must do 15 push-ups and 32 sit-ups, each set in one minute.

The swimming test is one exam that is especially hard and exhausting. It has several parts. Recruits must first jump off a platform 5 feet (1.5 m) high and then swim 328 feet (100 m)—a little less distance than the length of a football field. They must also tread water for five minutes. Passing this test means recruits will be ready for any Coast Guard operation at sea.

Recruits during their water-treading test

Graduation Day

Recruits are ready to graduate when they pass all their tests. During graduation, each company marches in a special parade in front of family members who attend the event. Once the graduation ceremony ends, each seaman recruit is officially a Guardian.

Seamen recruits stand at attention during their graduation ceremony.

During training, the recruits choose what they want to do after graduation. Some go straight to work where they will learn on the job, such as those who decide to become part of a search-and-rescue team. Others, like John Patrone, go to a Coast Guard school for special skills training. John trained to be a **boatswain's mate**—someone who is in charge of a ship's crew or equipment. No matter what they end up doing, all Guardians follows the U.S. Coast Guard's **motto** "Always Ready" and serve their country proudly!

Members of the U.S. Coast Guard serve the country in important ways, from stopping criminal activity along shores to rescuing boaters at sea.

All jobs in the U.S. Coast Guard are open to women as well as men.

Preparing for the Coast Guard

You may be interested in joining the Coast Guard someday. You can prepare now by doing well in school, keeping your body in top physical shape, and being a good person. The following rules also apply:

- ★ You must be between 17 and 27 years old.
- ★ You must be a citizen of the United States, or be a **legal immigrant** who is approved to live in the United States permanently.
- ★ You should have a high school diploma or general **equivalency** diploma (GED). In some cases, the Coast Guard will accept an enlisted person without a high school diploma or GED.
- ★ You must pass a Coast Guard job skills test and a physical exam.
- ★ It is best if you know how to swim, although it is not a requirement before beginning basic training.

Glossary

armed forces (ARMD FORSS-iz) the military groups a country uses to protect itself; in the United States these are the Army, the Navy, the Air Force, the Marines, and the Coast Guard

boatswain's mate (BOH-suhnz MAYT) a person who is in charge of the crew or equipment on a ship

civilians (si-VIL-yuhnz) people who are not members of the armed forces

coast (KOHST) land that runs along an ocean

commander (kuh-MAN-duhr) someone in the armed forces who is in charge of a group of people

company (KUHM-puh-nee) a group of Coast Guard recruits who are going through basic training together

conditioning (kuhn-DISH-uh-ning) working out to stay in shape

douse (DOUSS) to soak with water

drill (DRIL) a military training exercise, such as firing a weapon, that is practiced over and over

enlisting (en-LIST-ing) joining a branch of the armed forces

equivalency (i-KWIV-uh-luhn-see) being equal in value or significance

Guardian (GAR-dee-uhn) someone who is a member of the U.S. Coast Guard

legal immigrant (LEE-guhl IM-uh-gruhnt) a person who lawfully comes from one country to live permanently in a new one

motto (MOT-oh) a saying that states what someone believes in

nautical (NAW-tuh-kuhl) having to do with ships or sailing

navigate (NAV-uh-gayt) to guide a ship on the sea

pace (PAYSS) the speed at which someone does something

pistol (PISS-tuhl) a small gun

processing (PROSS-ess-ing) an organized series of activities that recruits go through, such as filling out paperwork and getting medical exams, before they begin their basic training

ranks (RANGKS) official military positions or levels

seaman recruits (SEE-muhn ri-KROOTS) enlisted men and women who are going through basic training in the Coast Guard

smuggling (SMUHG-ling) bringing goods into a country illegally

stranded (STRAND-id) left in a strange or unpleasant place

treading (TRED-ing) swimming in one place while your body is in a vertical position in the water

Index

Cape May, New Jersey 7, 8, 18
company commander 10–11, 12
enlistment rules 22
firefighting 4–5, 14
graduating 20–21
gun training 16–17
Helmsman, The 15
jobs 21
navigating 14
Patrone, John 5, 6–7, 21
physical training 12–13, 14
processing 9, 10
Sig Sauer P229 16–17
swimming 13, 18–19, 22
tests 18–19, 20
tying knots 14
values 15

Bibliography

Gray, Judy Silverstein. *The U.S. Coast Guard and Military Careers.* Berkeley Heights, NJ: Enslow (2008).

Paradis, Adrian A. *Opportunities in Military Careers.* New York: McGraw-Hill (2006).

Read More

David, Jack. *United States Coast Guard.* Minneapolis, MN: Bellwether Media (2008).

Dolan, Edward F. *Careers in the U.S. Coast Guard.* New York: Benchmark (2010).

Learn More Online

To learn more about the U.S. Coast Guard, visit
www.bearportpublishing.com/BecomingaSoldier

About the Author

Meish Goldish has written more than 200 books for children.
He lives in Brooklyn, New York.